You Are in Roman Britain

Ivan Minnis

www.raintreepublishers.co.uk

Visit our website to find out more information about **Raintree** books.

To order:
☎ Phone 44 (0) 1865 888112
🖹 Send a fax to 44 (0) 1865 314091
💻 Visit the Raintree Bookshop at **www.raintreepublishers.co.uk** to browse our catalogue and order online.

First published in Great Britain by Raintree, Halley Court, Jordan Hill, Oxford OX2 8EJ, part of Harcourt Education.
Raintree is a registered trademark of Harcourt Education Ltd.

Editorial: Nick Hunter and Catherine Clarke
Design: Michelle Lisseter, Richard Parker and Celia Floyd
Illustrations: Jeff Edwards
Picture Research: Maria Joannou and Ginny Stroud-Lewis
Production: Kevin Blackman

Originated by Dot Gradations Ltd
Printed and bound in China by South China Printing Company

ISBN 1 844 43287 4
08 07 06 05 04
10 9 8 7 6 5 4 3 2 1

British Library Cataloguing in Publication Data
Minnis, Ivan
You Are in Roman Britain. – (You Are There)
936.1'04
A full catalogue record for this book is available from the British Library.

Acknowledgements
The publishers would like to thank the following for permission to reproduce photographs:
AKG images (Justus Gopel) p. **24**; Alamy Images (Finnbarr) p. **6**; Ancient Art and Architecture pp. **7** (R. Sheridan), **9** (R. Sheridan), **13**, **15**, **16**, **18** (R. Sheridan), **19** (Brian Wilson), **20**, **23**, **25** (R. Sheridan), **26** (R. Sheridan), **27**, **29** (R. Sheridan); Bath and Northeast Somerset Council p. **10**; Corbis pp. **12** (Polypix; Eye Ubiquitous), **28** (Araldo de Luca); John Seely pp. **8**, **14**; Terry Griffiths and Magnet Harlequin pp. **5**, **17**, **22**; Trevor Clifford p. **11**.

Cover photograph of a mosaic from Fishbourne Roman Palace and Gardens, reproduced with permission of Kate Shemilt.

Contents

Any words appearing in bold, **like this**, are explained
in the Glossary.

The Roman Empire

There were many **civilizations** around the world 2000 years ago. In Central America, the Zapotecs and Mayans ruled large areas of land. In Asia, China was growing strong. Around the Mediterranean Sea, the great civilizations of ancient Egypt and Greece had become part of the Roman **Empire**.

In 700 BC, Rome was a small town, but it began to take over other lands as it grew rich. By the time the Roman **Emperor** Claudius invaded Britain in AD 43, Rome had **conquered** much of Europe. Soon, most of England and Wales were under Roman control. The Romans named this new addition *Britannia*.

In AD 100, the Roman Empire controlled many other lands, including Britain.

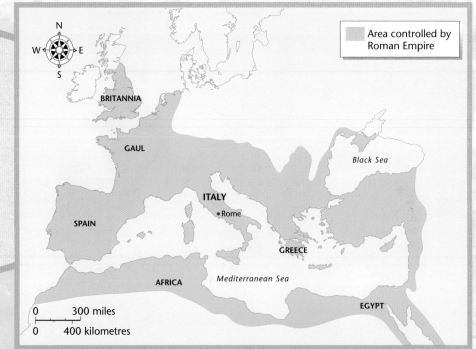

Area controlled by Roman Empire

N W E S

BRITANNIA

GAUL

Black Sea

ITALY

• Rome

SPAIN

GREECE

AFRICA   *Mediterranean Sea*

EGYPT

0   300 miles
0   400 kilometres

Hadrian's Wall stretched for 118 kilometres (73 miles) along the border between England and Scotland.

Hadrian's Wall

The Romans never captured Scotland. Instead, in AD 122, Emperor Hadrian ordered a wall to be built to stop Scottish tribes attacking Roman towns. The wall had many **forts** and soldiers to guard it. You can still see Hadrian's Wall today.

Roman Britain

In this book you will travel back in time to Roman Britain. You will see what life was like at the time of Emperor Hadrian, who ruled from AD 117 to 138. You will take a walk through the busy towns, meet the people and find out how they lived and worked.

The conquest of Britain

A Roman army first came to Britain in 55 BC. A great general, Julius Caesar, raided the country but did not stay to make it part of the **Empire**. Nearly 100 years later, in AD 43, **Emperor** Claudius sent an army to invade. The **Celtic** tribes who lived in England were easily beaten.

In AD 60, Queen Boudicca led the British **revolt** against the Roman invaders. The tribes fought hard, but the Roman army was too strong. Soon, the Romans were in total control.

Boudicca and her daughters fought the Romans from her war chariot.

The Romans built forts all over Britain. These are the remains of one built at Chester.

Settling in Britain

The Romans soon began to make Britain like other parts of their Empire. They built good roads so soldiers could march quickly around the country. For the first time, towns appeared around Britain. **Forts** were also built. This made sure that there were always soldiers ready if the tribes decided to fight back. Britain was to be ruled by Rome for over 350 years.

The ancient Romans

Imagine making your way through the crowds on a busy street in Roman Britain. You can see people from all over the **Empire**. Roman soldiers march past in their armour. Roman officials wear long cloaks called togas. Rich women wear dresses called stolas. Stolas are many different colours. The rich women also wear make-up, perfume and fine jewellery.

The Celts

In Britain, the Romans need warm cloaks. The weather is much colder than in Rome.

Wealthy Romans often have paintings on the walls of their homes. These show them in their finest clothes.

The Celts lived in Britain before the Romans invaded. They are used to the weather. Celtic men wear warm woollen trousers. Women wear woollen robes and shawls. Some Romans copy the Celtic tribes and wear trousers.

Slaves

There are many **slaves** in Roman Britain. They come from all over the Empire. Many of them have been captured in battle. Slaves can be bought and sold by their owners. They work for rich Romans – in their homes or on the land.

The Celts are skilled metal workers. This statue shows a blacksmith at work.

Roman towns

The Romans have built towns across Britain. The biggest is Londinium (London). In the centre of a town you will find the **forum**. This is where everyone comes to buy and sell their goods. People also come here to hold meetings and talk to friends.

There are other important public buildings. There are **temples** where the Romans worship their gods. Bathhouses are always full. The rich go there to relax and meet their friends, as well as to wash.

People travel from all over the Empire to visit the warm baths at Aquae Sulis (Bath).

Roman cities are built around the forum. The biggest forum of all is in Rome.

Finding out about towns: Silchester

The Romans built the town of Calleva. Unlike many other Roman towns, it has never been built over. This means that we can learn a lot from the ruins. People have found many beautiful **mosaics** as well as everyday objects. Calleva is now called Silchester.

Busy streets

Be careful crossing the street. The streets are not always clean. Horses and cattle pull heavy carts to bring goods in and out of the city. The wet British weather means that the streets can get very muddy. Some streets have stepping stones to keep your feet out of the animal dung!

In the countryside

In the countryside, farmers grow food for the people in the towns. Many different crops are grown around the **Empire**. In Italy and north Africa, the weather is hot and dry. Here olives are grown for their oil, and grapes to make wine. In Britain, the weather is cooler and damper. Vegetables such as cabbages and carrots are grown. Cattle and sheep are kept for meat. Cattle also provide milk. Sheeps' wool is used to make warm clothes. Children often look after the sheep on the hillsides.

There are Roman villas, or farms, all over Britain. This one is in Gloucestershire.

Oxen, such as those in this bronze statue, pull heavy ploughs for the farmers.

Life on the farm

Many farms are owned by rich **landowners**. They live in huge **villas**. All of the hard work is done by poor farm workers and **slaves**. Ploughs pulled by oxen are used to prepare the ground for sowing the seeds. At **harvest** time, the farm workers spend all day harvesting the crop by hand. Sometimes, the whole family has to work in the fields.

A Roman feast

Most Roman families eat very simple meals. Women manage the households. They are experts at making sure that no food is wasted. You might have lentils and beans, which are made into a stew and eaten with bread. You will not eat meat very often as it is expensive. Storing food is a problem. There are no fridges in Roman Britain. Strong-tasting sauces are used by cooks to cover the taste of stale food.

The Romans cook over charcoal, a bit like a modern barbecue.

Wealthy Romans feast on all kinds of fine foods. This mosaic shows just some of them.

Fine food

The food eaten by the rich is very different. They only eat one main meal per day, but this is often a great feast. It starts at around four o'clock in the afternoon and can last many hours. People eat lying on couches around a table. **Slaves** prepare several courses. Venison from deer is a popular dish for the rich in Britain. You may be offered dormouse cooked in honey. New foods such as spices, figs, olives and grapes have been brought to Britain from warmer parts of the **Empire**.

Life for children

If you are from a poor family you will not go to school. You cannot spend much time playing, though. Children are expected to work from a very early age. Even a four-year-old is expected to do their share, perhaps by gathering stray ears of corn at **harvest** time.

Life for a rich child is easier. Boys and some girls are sent to primary school. They are expected to learn things by heart and can be punished for making mistakes. The only schools are in the largest towns. In the countryside, **slaves** who can read and write might teach the children of the rich. Girls do not go to school after the age of twelve. They are taught how to run a home by their mothers.

If you are lucky enough to have time to play, you might play ball games like this.

Only important people can write on paper, using pens like this and ink made from soot.

Reading and writing

Many different languages are spoken in Roman Britain. None is like modern English. The Roman language is Latin. It is spoken by **scholars** and important people. If you learn to write Latin, you will use a special pen called a stylus to scratch letters on to **wax tablets**. The tablets can be melted down and used again.

Roman art

Across Roman Britain, you can see that many public buildings are decorated with statues and carvings. Roman **emperors** like to have statues of themselves in the cities. They show the people how powerful they are. **Temples** have images of the gods who are worshipped there. The public baths may have statues and **mosaics** of Neptune, god of the sea.

Mosaic pictures like this one are made up of hundreds of tiny pieces of coloured tile. This Roman mosaic is in Sussex.

Art at home

If you enter the house of a wealthy family, you will see art all around you. **Villas** often have beautiful floors covered with mosaics. Mosaics are pictures made with lots of tiny coloured tiles. Different scenes are painted on the walls of wealthy homes.

Finding out about silver

Many beautiful things are made of silver. Silver used to be mined in Britain. It was one of the reasons why the Romans decided to invade.

Builders and technology

Everyone in Britain is amazed by the huge stone buildings put up by the Romans. Builders use simple tools like hammers, chisels and saws. Some of the grandest buildings are the **temples** and public baths in the towns. Most other buildings are made from wood.

In the homes of the rich, there is even central heating! Hot air is passed through spaces under the floors and in gaps in the walls. A **slave** keeps the **furnace** hot. This keeps the Romans warm during the British winters.

In an underground heating system, stone pillars hold up the floor so that warm air can pass underneath.

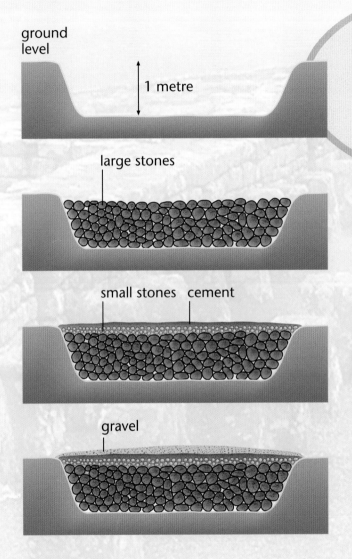

ground level

1 metre

large stones

small stones   cement

gravel

The Romans build roads by digging a ditch and then filling it with layers of stones, gravel and cement.

Finding out about technology

Many Roman buildings and roads were built so well that we can still see them today, 2000 years later. They tell us that Roman technology was very advanced for its time.

Roman roads

Roman roads run from one end of Britain to the other. They are used to move soldiers quickly around the country. Roman roads have fairly smooth surfaces so carts do not get stuck. They are always as straight as possible. Trees and bushes are cleared on either side so robbers have nowhere to hide.

Having fun

Everyone gets very excited when the games are on at the local **amphitheatre**. This is a Roman sports stadium. You pay to watch **gladiators** fight to the death! They fight against other gladiators and wild animals such as lions and bears. Sand covers the floor of the stadium to soak up the blood of the gladiators. When a gladiator is beaten, the crowd can decide whether he lives or dies.

Gladiators fight each other or wild animals to entertain the crowds at the amphitheatre.

seating for audience   stage

Roman theatres, such as this one at St. Albans, are open to the air – so bad weather can cause problems.

Going to the theatre

There are more peaceful types of entertainment. Many people go to the theatre to watch plays and mimes. Roman actors always wear masks. The faces show the type of person they are playing. You might see a pantomime. This is a special type of play where one person tells a story while another acts it out through dance and mime. Most actors are men. Women sometimes act in short mimes.

Not everyone can go to the theatre. People who live in the country may be a long way from the nearest town. They have to make their own fun. Board games are popular.

Roman rulers

The Roman **Empire** is very large and needs strong leaders to keep control of it. It is ruled by an **emperor**. He is helped by a group of powerful men called the **senate**. They meet at the **forum** in Rome to talk about important matters. Parts of the Empire like Britain are ruled by a governor, who is sent from Rome.

As well as the governor, public officials run each town in Britain. Many of these come from Rome but some are local people. They accept Roman rule and live like wealthy Romans.

Julius Caesar is the most famous Roman general. He led an army to Britain in 55 BC.

The Roman army

The Roman army is the toughest army in the world. If you meet a soldier, or legionary, he will tell you stories about the battles he has fought in faraway lands. The army is divided into **legions** of around 4000–6000 men. Some legionaries have married local women and settled in Britain.

Roman soldiers wear armour on their bodies and fight with swords and daggers.

Roman religion

The Romans have many different gods. Each one is said to look after a certain part of people's lives. One goddess, Cardea, is the goddess of door hinges! Each god has its own **temples** and priests. The priests make sure the gods are kept happy by offering **sacrifices**. Even the **emperor** brings animals and food to offer to the gods.

When they add a new place to the **Empire**, the Romans make sure to include its local gods in their worship. The huge temple of Sulis Minerva in Bath honours the Roman goddess Minerva and the **Celtic** god Sulis.

You might see small statues like this one, if you are in the home of a wealthy Roman. This statue shows Mars, the god of war.

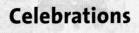
This Roman mosaic is in Dorset. It shows Jesus Christ.

Finding out about religion

Religion in Roman Britain changed over time. In AD 313, Constantine became the first Christian emperor. Christian **mosaics** have been found from Roman Britain. They tell us that many other Romans were also Christians.

Celebrations

There are many festivals to celebrate throughout the year. In April, there are bonfires and parties to celebrate the founding of Rome. In August, **slaves** get a day off in honour of the goddess Diana.

Facts for Roman Britain

Now you know about Roman Britain and its people. Here are a few other things you need to know to get by while the Romans are in power:

Numbers

The Romans use letters to write numbers. Here are some important numbers:

I	= 1	VIII	=	8
II	= 2	IX	=	9
III	= 3	X	=	10
IV	= 4	L	=	50
V	= 5	C	=	100
VI	= 6	D	=	500
VII	= 7	M	=	1000

Measures

Measuring accurately was very important in the great buildings the Romans built:

1 *uncia* = 2.46 centimetres = 1 Roman inch

1 *pes* = 29.5 centimetres = 1 Roman foot

1 *passus* = 1.48 metres = 1 Roman pace

1 *mille* = 1480 metres = 1 Roman mile.

You need to know about weights and measures when you go shopping. This is a pharmacy.

January is named after the god Janus. His two faces look back to the old year, and forward to the new.

Months of the year

January = *Januarius* – named after Janus, god of gateways

February = *Februarius* – from *februare*, which means 'to purify'

March = *Martius* – named after Mars, the god of war

April = *Aprilis* – from *aperire*, which means 'to open', the way flowers open in spring

May = *Maius* – named after Maia, goddess of spring

June = *Junius* – named after Juno, queen of the gods

July = *Julius* – named after Julius Caesar (this is the month of his birth)

August = *Augustus* – named in honour of **Emperor** Augustus

September = September – the seventh month

October = October – the eighth month

November = November – the ninth month

December = December – the tenth month

Find out for yourself

Unfortunately, you cannot travel back in time to Roman Britain, but you can still find out about the ancient Romans and how they lived. You will find the answers to some of your questions in this book. You can also use other books and the Internet.

Books to read

Heritage: The Romans in Britain, Robert Hull (Hodder Wayland, 1999)
History Starts Here: The Ancient Romans, Anita Ganeri (Hodder Wayland, 2003)
I Wonder Why Romans Wore Togas and Other Questions About Ancient Rome, Fiona MacDonald (Kingfisher Books, 1997)

Using the Internet

Explore the Internet to find out more about Roman Britain. Websites can change, but if one of the links below no longer works, don't worry. Use a search engine such as www.yahooligans.com and type in keywords such as 'Roman **villa**', 'Hadrian's Wall', 'Roman army' and 'Julius Caesar'.

Websites

http://www.bbc.co.uk/schools/romans
Take a look at this interactive guide to Roman Britain.
http://www.romanbaths.co.uk
Go on a virtual tour of the Roman bathouse at Bath – both past and present!

Disclaimer
All the Internet addresses (URLs) given in this book were valid at the time of going to press. However, due to the dynamic nature of the Internet, some addresses may have changed, or sites may have ceased to exist since publication. While the author and publishers regret any inconvenience this may cause readers, no responsibility for any such changes can be accepted by either the author or the publishers

Glossary

amphitheatre round building like a stadium with seats around a central space or stage. Romans go to the amphitheatre to watch gladiator games.

Celtic of, or to do with, the Celts. The Celts were a people that lived in Britain at the time the Romans invaded.

civilization united group of people living together

conquer to take over control of a country and its people

emperor ruler of Rome

empire large area of land ruled by the Romans, including parts of Europe, north Africa and the Middle East

fort building with high walls and few windows that the soldiers who live there can easily defend

forum market place or public meeting area in a Roman town

furnace structure where useful heat is produced. Furnace fires are kept hot to give central heating to wealthy Roman homes.

gladiator trained fighter who uses a sword or other weapon to entertain crowds in fights to the death

harvest gathering of the season's crops

landowner wealthy person paid rent by the farmers working on their land

legion Roman army unit made up of 4000 to 6000 soldiers

mosaic pattern or picture made up from small pieces of coloured tile, glass or stone

revolt stand up to, or fight against the rulers of a country

sacrifice offering of animals or food to the gods

scholar educated man in ancient Rome. Scholars can read and write Latin.

senate group of men who meet to decide laws

slave person held captive and forced to work

temple place where gods or goddesses are worshipped

villa large Roman house, with buildings arranged around a courtyard

wax tablet sheet of wax used for writing on before, or instead of, paper

Index

Titles in the *You Are There* series include:

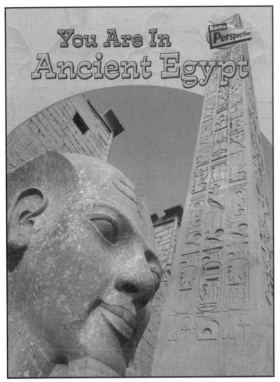

Hardback   1 844 43285 8

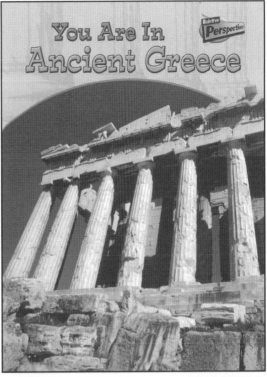

Hardback   1 844 43286 6

Hardback   1 844 43287 4

Hardback   1 844 43288 2

Find out about the other titles in this series on our website www.raintreepublishers.co.uk